Buttons for General Washington

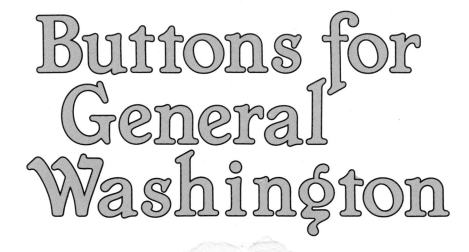

For Rob - I hope you enjoy John's story.

Buttons for General Washington

by Peter and Connie Roop
illustrated by
Peter E. Hanson

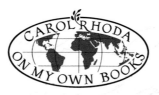

Carolrhoda Books · Minneapolis, Minnesota

For Father—a patriotic son of the American Revolution whose heritage enhances our history

This book is available in two editions:
Library binding by Carolrhoda Books, Inc.
Soft cover by First Avenue Editions, 1997
c/o The Lerner Group
241 First Avenue North
Minneapolis, Minnesota 55401

LIBRARY OF CONGRESS CATALOGING-IN-PUBLICATION DATA

Roop, Peter.
    Buttons for General Washington.

    (A Carolrhoda on my own book)
    Summary: Reconstructs a possible mission of the fourteen-year-old spy who carried messages to George Washington's camp in the buttons of his coat during the Revolutionary War.
    1. Darragh, John—Juvenile literature. 2. United States—History—Revolution, 1775-1783—Secret service—Juvenile literature. 3. Washington, George, 1732-1799—Friends and associates—Juvenile literature. 4. Spies—United States—Biography—Juvenile literature. [1. Darragh, John. 2. Spies. 3. United States—Revolution, 1775-1783—Secret service] I. Roop, Connie. II. Hanson, Peter E., ill. III. Title. IV. Series.
E280.D37R67 1986   973.3'85   [92]   86-6120
ISBN 0-87614-294-3 (lib. bdg.)
ISBN 0-87614-476-8 (pbk.)

Manufactured in the United States of America
    12 13 14 15 16 – P/SP – 02 01 00 99 98

AUTHORS' NOTE

Spies played an important role in the Revolutionary War. American spies kept General George Washington informed about the size of British troops and the state of their supplies, and they often discovered when and where the British planned to attack.

In the fall of 1777, the British army, under the command of General Howe, had captured and occupied Philadelphia. The Darragh family lived across the street from General Howe's British headquarters. As Quakers, the Darraghs were gentle people who used "thee," "thy," and "thou" as forms of address, dressed plainly, and opposed violence. They were not supposed to fight on either side, but Charles, the oldest Darragh boy, had joined General Washington's army, and the rest of the family became spies to aid in his safety.

Mr. Darragh, a teacher, created a code for secret messages. Mrs. Darragh, who later became the most famous spy of the family, hid the messages in the buttons of her son John's coat. Fourteen-year-old John then took the messages to Washington's camp, where Charles Darragh read them.

This story tells what might have happened on one of John Darragh's dangerous missions as an American spy.

"Are any soldiers in the street, John?"
his mother asked.
"Only the guard at General Howe's
headquarters," John answered.
"Remember, John.
Keep away from the British soldiers,"
his mother said.
"And go the way I told thee."
"But I know a faster way,"
John said.
"Do as thy mother asks,"
his father said.
"She has sent messages to
General Washington before."

John nodded his head.
He wished that his mother would
finish sewing the new buttons
on his coat.
He was nervous and in a hurry
to be on his way to
General Washington's camp.

"Here, John," his mother said at last.
"The new buttons look
just like the old ones."
John took his coat.
He ran his fingers over
the cloth-covered buttons.
He could not feel the small holes
inside the buttons.
Secret messages for General Washington
were hidden in those holes.

"If I am caught, will anyone
be able to read the messages?"
John asked.
"No," answered his father.
"I wrote them in a code that
only thy brother Charles can read."
"I wish I could give the buttons
to General Washington himself,"
John said.
"Maybe someday thee will,"
his mother said.
John carefully buttoned his coat.
"Be careful," his father warned.
"The British are looking
for American spies."

"If they catch thee, it means prison—
or worse," his mother said.
A shiver ran down John's back.

He knew that captured spies
were lucky to end up in prison.
Usually they were hanged.
"I will be careful," John said.
"Here is thy pass to leave
Philadelphia," his mother said.
"Thou needs it to get
past the British guards."

John put the pass in his pocket.
His hands shook as he touched
the buttons for good luck.
"We will wait supper for thee,"
his mother said.
"Godspeed, John," his father said.

John walked up Second Street.
He turned on Market Street.
British soldiers were everywhere.

14

John wished they would all
go back to England.
John walked slower as he neared
the guardpost at the edge of town.

"Hey, Yankee Doodle," he heard
a voice call from behind him.
John turned quickly.
It was Samuel Baker.
Samuel's family liked
the British soldiers.
They wanted the British
to win the war.
The Bakers and other Tories
wanted America to be
part of England again.
John hated Samuel even more than
he hated the British soldiers.

"Did you see all of our new soldiers?"
Samuel asked.

"You Americans can never win now.
General Howe will whip Washington
before Christmas."

"He will not," John said fiercely.

"Oh, yes, he will," Samuel said.

"We British are too strong for you."
John stepped up to Samuel.

"Just thee wait and see who wins
the war," John said angrily.

"When we win, thee can return to
England where thou belongs!"

"Who is going to make me?"
Samuel said, poking John.

"Me!" John yelled.

Before John could move,

Samuel hit him hard in the stomach.

John fell down.

"See," Samuel said.

"We will win."

Samuel walked away proudly.

Brushing off his coat, John stood up.
He wished he could hit Samuel back,
even though he knew that
he should not fight.
Besides, he knew it was more important
to reach General Washington's camp.

John stopped at the guardpost.
A red-coated British soldier
took his pass.
He looked at it for a long time.
John began to worry.
"You are going to your aunt's house?"
the soldier asked.
"Yes," answered John.
"I must check each pass carefully,"
the soldier said.
"There are many American spies.
You are not a spy are you?"
the soldier asked with a smile.
"Oh, no, sir," John answered quickly.
"Off with you then," said the soldier.
"Just remember, we hang
any spies we catch."

Well, thou won't catch me, John thought
as he put the pass back in his pocket.

John knew he should not be too
sure of himself, though,
so he kept a sharp lookout
for more British soldiers.
They might guess that he was
a spy if they found him
past his aunt's house.
They might even find
the secret messages.

John stopped suddenly.
He heard horses coming.
He jumped over a ditch
and hid behind a tree.

Five British soldiers
came along the road.
They passed slowly.
They were looking for someone.

John waited until the soldiers
had ridden away.
He touched his buttons for good luck.
A button was missing!
John looked all over the ground.
He could not find the button anywhere.
Then he remembered Samuel Baker's blow.
The button must have come off
near the guardhouse.
John started to run back down the road
toward Philadelphia.
His breath came in short gasps.
He had to find that button.

He stopped near the guardpost.

He looked all around for the button.

"Are you back so soon?"

John jumped in surprise.

The British guard walked toward him.

"I lost one of my buttons," John said.

"My mother would not be happy
if I could not find it."

The soldier held out his hand.

He had John's button!
"I found it where you boys
were fighting," the soldier said.
John tried to keep his hands from
shaking as he took the button.
He hoped the soldier
had not found the message.
"Thank thee for finding my button,"
John said, backing away.
"On your way, then," said the soldier.

John put the button
deep in his pocket.
He looked at the sky.
It was past noon.
Against his mother's warning,
he took a shortcut through the woods
toward General Washington's camp.
John stopped for a rest after an hour.
He took a long drink from an icy stream.

Suddenly, a hand grabbed him from
behind as he stood up.
"What might you be doing in these
woods?" asked a gruff voice.
John was spun around
before he could answer.
He faced a bearded man.
The man aimed a pistol at John.

John said the first words
that came to him.

"I was hunting."

"Hunting without a gun?" the man asked.

"I was really going to my aunt's house,"
John said.

"I will take you with me to find out
the truth," the man said sharply.

"Now march," he ordered.

John knew that the man would
shoot him if he tried to run.

They walked through the woods
for a long time.

John was hungry and tired.

He was scared, too.

Where was the man taking him?

What would John do
if they were going to a British camp?

At last they came to an open field.
A large white tent stood in one corner.
Soldiers in blue uniforms
were marching in the field.
It was an American camp.

John breathed a sigh of relief.
Once he talked to Charles,
everything would be all right.
"We will have the truth from you now,"
the man told John.

He took John to the white tent.
"I have a spy here," the man told
a soldier guarding the tent.
"I caught him prowling
in the woods near Philadelphia."

The soldier stepped into the tent.
He was back within a moment.
"Bring him in."
The bearded man pushed John
into the tent.

"Sit down, son,"
said a tall man in a blue uniform.
John sat in a wooden chair.
"They tell me you are a spy,"
the man said.
"You are young for a spy.
Whose side do you spy for?"
"General Washington's side," John said.
"I am John Darragh.
Charles Darragh is my brother.
He helps General Washington.
Can I see Charles now?"
The man turned to the soldier.
"Send Charles Darragh to me at once."
John sat stiffly
in front of the uniformed man.
It seemed like a year
before Charles arrived.

"Why, John," Charles said in surprise.

John smiled.

Now he could prove

that he spied for Washington.

"Mother sent me.

I have some messages

for General Washington."

John took the loose button

from his pocket.

"There is a message in Father's code
hidden inside."
Charles uncovered the button.
He took out the message
and looked at it.
"Please decode the message right away,"
the tall man said.
"Don't, Charles," said John.
"Only General Washington
is supposed to know."

Charles laughed at his brother.

"John, this *is* General Washington."

General Washington held out his hand.

John shook it.

"It is an honor to shake the hand
of so brave a patriot,"
the General said.

"Thank thee, sir," John said.

"Charles," said the General,
"please report to me after you
have decoded the messages."

General Washington left the tent.

Charles began cutting the buttons
off John's coat.
John could not believe that he
had met General Washington.
Washington's words of praise
still filled John's ears.

After removing the messages,
Charles sewed the buttons
back on John's coat.
"Now be careful on the way home,"
Charles said.
"We need thee to bring more buttons."

John touched the buttons for good luck.
Then he laughed as he put on his coat.
"I will bring enough buttons for
General Washington's whole army!"